T0161055

STAY
SAFE

EMMA HINE

SARABANDE BOOKS  Louisville, KY

Library of Congress Cataloging-in-Publication Data

Names: Hine, Emma, author.
Title: Stay safe : poems / by Emma Hine.
Description: First edition. | Louisville, KY : Sarabande Books, 2021
Identifiers: LCCN 2019048499 (print) | LCCN 2019048500 (e-book)
ISBN 9781946448682 (paperback) | ISBN 9781946448699 (e-book)
Subjects: LCSH: Families—Poetry. | Grief—Poetry.
Classification: LCC PS3608.I554 S73 2021 (print)
LCC PS3608.I554 (e-book) | DDC 811/.6—dc23
LC record available at https://lccn.loc.gov/2019048499
LC e-book record available at https://lccn.loc.gov/2019048500

Cover and interior design by Alban Fischer.
Printed in Canada.
This book is printed on acid-free paper.
Sarabande Books is a nonprofit literary organization.

This project is supported in part by an award from the National
Endowment for the Arts. The Kentucky Arts Council, the state
arts agency, supports Sarabande Books with state tax dollars and
federal funding from the National Endowment for the Arts.

FOR MY PARENTS

AND MY SISTERS

Contents

Introduction

The most beautiful music is the music of what happens.

—IRISH PROVERB

What a pleasure and a revelation it was to find Emma Hine's *Stay Safe*, a book that tells a fascinating overarching story, while exploring the richness of narrative in individual poems, all without the wink and the nod of contemporary self-reflexivity. Using a kind of recursive strategy, Hine tells her stories, and retells them, from differing points of view and different lives. Some of the stories are "literal," convincing as straightforward events from the poet's history, containing a wealth of palpable detail. But there are also abrupt, associative turns and gaps within these poems; it's only after we sit quietly a moment after reading that we realize the turns and gaps contain nine-tenths of the matter. Other poems employ dreams, or dreams within dreams, or imaginings, as in the amazing "Selkie," in which the eldest tells her younger sisters their mother was once a seal, who only came to land to discover "what it felt like to be lost." Over time the mother repeatedly left her ocean family and one day discovered her "pelt" was missing, so had to stay on land, sleeping under the boardwalk and finding, one by one, her three daughters, hidden under flowers or in other odd places. Years later, after the narrator has almost forgotten this story herself, she is on the beach with her sisters when they approach her holding a brine-soaked piece of cardboard they claim is their mother's pelt. It is difficult to describe the unique mixture of grief and enchantment this poem evokes in the reader. In any case, it is a feeling that rises out of many others in the book.

Hine does not neglect image or sound for the sake of story—her talent is wide enough to include all. This image, for example, from the remarkable poem sequence "Flight Path":

> The fuselage burned so hot I could see right through
> into the cockpit where a young woman sat
> impossibly aflame, like a keyhole, or
> an exit, or a torch into the tunnel-end of risk.

Or this, about a pilot crashed and sinking to the ocean bottom:

> His organs cast
> dim shadows on the clear walls of his skin.

As to *Stay Safe*'s pleasures for the ear, here is one of many from "Keeping":

> by then too I saw moons
> everywhere, in the web-whorls
> spiders left on the windows,
> in the pale grubs curled in the dirt.

We may read the book as the story of three sisters and their parents, everywhere accompanied by a persistent sense of dislocation and imminent loss. We learn early on that the family moves often, leaving a trail of houses behind like empty shells. And the mother herself is not "safe"—she has a brain tumor, and one of her repeated counsels to the sisters is that they *take care of each other*. She needn't worry—throughout the book the sisters are close by each other and seem in some ways hardly separate. Even in "Echo Hotel," the sci-fi prose poem sequence, where a narrator, along with her father and mother, is on a self-replenishing spaceship continuously wandering through the universe, we find a "cluster of sisters gripping each other tightly in case the darkness tries to tear them apart."

Many of the poems have their life in or nearby water; others are set in the air. Hine is intimately conversant with the technical details of human flight. As in the quote from "Flight Path," fire also plays a role ("a young woman sat / impossibly aflame"). The only missing element is earth, and in fact the planet itself seems most alien to the poet and her family, their true home in or beneath the ocean, afloat in midair, or in space. The earth explicitly makes the most memorable appearance in the book, and that, seen from a spaceship: "a tiny blue orb like the coin of light at the top of a very deep well."

The equation of *sisters, mother, family*, with *air, water, fire*, along with the dreamy manipulation of these elements, lend the poems the uncanniness of fairy tales. And as with fairy tales, *Stay Safe* sees with the wonder and ebullience of a child, even as it understands with the psychological sophistication of one who has grieved adult losses and made it through. It is a book of its time that nevertheless finds its place outside trends, or schools, or modes. It is a startling debut—enchanted, and enchanting.

—Jeffrey Skinner and Sarah Gorham, 2019

Don't You See

Sometimes when I tell it they fall
and their parents find them twitching
like wrens on the flagstones, grieving
over wings that didn't work. Oh well.
In other versions the children do better,
and rise with the boy above town
still dressed for sleep, while their shadows
dive across the roofs below.
In the towns that this boy visits,
the people are afraid of geese—
of looking up at high dark shapes
that might be nightgowned children
flying away. In some towns, the boy
is not even a boy at all, but a goose
in search of a flock. They say
he's living on an island where winter
never comes. That's where he takes
the children. They nest in the dunes
and are only afraid of the ticking sound
of the clock, which the boy says
was swallowed long ago by a creature
that swam up from the depths. Back home
their parents would point at the moon

and say that everyone falls asleep
under the same sky. On the island
they learn that everyone stays awake
to the same clock. *Don't you see,*
the clock says to the children,
you could stay in this place forever.
Don't you see, the clocks say to their families,
this is the beginning of a very long time.

Young Relics

They broke into houses,
my sisters—the empty ones,
just built, where nobody had yet
tried to sleep. Little mounds
of sawdust still in the corners,
no floorboards loose.
I imagine them there the way
I've seen them be with horses,
hands gentle on the walls—after all,
a house must learn to hold a family
with all its quivering systems
of energy and grief. I once saw Sierra
with a colt that wasn't ready
to be ridden. She stood in the stall
and talked until his heart rate slowed.
All through our neighborhood
new houses were dark and panicking.
Enter sisters.
Bringing comfort where it wasn't
supposed to be, no key for entry,
no light allowed, just a ritual gift

for the rooms alone to remember:

hands on their painted flanks.

Voices in the eaves.

Spring Break at Port Aransas

The boys I met told me to stay where the tide
had left the sand taut. The rarest shrimp lived there,
so small I couldn't see them, and if I bored enough holes

with the PVC pipe they'd given me, I'd harvest something
invisible. The narrow wells I dug resettled slowly,
a line trailing behind me up the beach. There was so much

on either side, rattlesnakes in the dunes, oil rigs shuddering
on the horizon. Sierra and Juliett, twins, shrieked when anything—
seaweed, fingers—touched them underwater. Something sharp

sliced through our mother's heel. On the last day we drove
to the souvenir store for hermit crabs, the kind
that cringe into their painted shells when a finger prods in.

We parked beside a yellow jeep. While my family crossed
the pavement, I stood briefly in the space between the cars.
There was a woman's torso drawn on the jeep's bright door:

thick black lines marked the weight of her breasts. Her nipples sprouted like sand dollars. My face was level with where her face should have been. Below the sargassum of her pubic hair, someone had written, *Show me yours.*

Red Planet

All Mars can see, bolted in place,
is the sky. She recites, *Red sky at night, sailor's
delight,* until her atmosphere shimmers.
She wants to be visible from everywhere,
      the brightest storm brewing

in this big wide sea. She converts sensations
into units of distance and units of force,
so that each time a body collides with her,
she can add it to her catalogue of impact:
      where, how hard,

how long the tremor. She lifts the oxide dust
gently from a crater and says, *Asteroid
at an oblique angle, seventy-eight miles across.*
She does this just by feel. No looking.
      Which might be why

she so loves the probes. When they land,
she goes as still as she can, so they won't startle
and unlatch. She wants them always charting
her shoal plains. When one enters
      her gravity too slowly

and bounces away, she wonders what
went wrong. She imagines it lost
out there, how it wanted her but couldn't
    touch her, or stay.

Grave Offerings

When I was still young enough, my mother told me
about the city at the great river's headwaters:

every building was a palace and in every palace
lived a king. Any time a king died

his family dismantled his throne to build
a funeral barge, which they filled with cracked vases,

blunt weapons, vellum maps soaked in ink.
On each prow they hung an emblem

of their king's particular death—the metal cast
of a scorpion, bouquet of teeth from a beast.

Then they floated the small ships down the river,
past cities like our own where the people talked

about the shrouded men passing by. This king
with the charred ivory figures must have kept horses

and died in a fire. This king never listened to his family.
This king went wild under a horn-tailed moon. And so,

my mother said, the kings live on in stories,
and who would ever know if the stories are true?

A Circling

Impossible to think of Frank and not think *shark*.

His bathrobe flopped open once, and there it was,

bite of thigh missing, skin like a spider tried

to stop the hole with web. I never looked at him

directly again. My mother fixed him lunch

while I stared anywhere but the carved space

that was the scar that was Frank. He was my great-uncle.

In the family story, his father tells him not to take a swim—

the shark net is down. Everyone knows not to swim

without the net. He dives from the cliff. From the air, a fin.

His flesh unlaces. There are teeth embedded in his bone.

By the time he died, I'd memorized his shape in the recliner,

the pattern of beer bottles across his floor. Mapping

his aftermath like a frontier. The shark hovers inches

above its own shadow. Frank pulls off his clothes in the sun.

Tornado Warning in Horse Country

*

The MRI revealed our mother's skull
a halo, the growth a drop of water
that may not splash.

This was the time of year when the wind plucked roofs
off well-built houses and left their inner workings
exposed to the sky.

She taped on the fridge a list
of everything she thought she hadn't taught us:

Expect sometimes to be lonely.
Take care of each other.
Don't live too much in the past.

She stood us in the mirror and showed
where they would cut. Through her new buzz,
her finger left a path like someone lost in wheat.

*

If it comes to it, my father said,
people will let out their horses.

My imagined filly was terrified,
her lungs rioting on wet pink wings.

He said, *They'll run for ditches and gullies.*
They know how to survive.

I'd already read the books that end,
beloved pony gets loose in a storm,
breaks a fetlock, mercy, *bang.*

After this the girl is never quite the same.

We drove on and watched for corkscrews
in the heavy line of clouds, him with his dear promises,
me with my selfish almost-thoughts:

maybe someday I'd have horses to let out,
would they find a low place for safety,
would I find them after,
would they be wounded somehow,
could I perform the kind and terrible thing?

Distortion for Afterward

When my neighbor's son hanged himself
from the tree in his yard, I was on my way home,
and he was a stencil dissolving
in the red-blue pulse of the trauma unit.
The leaves tilted purple above him,
the earth a sick green, as if with his sudden rupture
came a broader, more permanent shift:
physics resettling from the shock
into wrong answers. Every night after,
his mother set out candles in a ceremony
recalling bedtime, the ritual of sleep.
But on that first night, her voice carried
into all the houses, welled under my door,
not isolated words but the keen
of molecules changing their structure,
washing into my bedroom where I sat awake,
my robe on the hook now a lolling navy tongue,
my furniture jolting inward, bumping me,
telling me to nail it to the walls.

Selkie

AFTER BRIGIT PEGEEN KELLY

I told my sisters our mother was born
in the ocean. What was the harm? I told them
she was a seal. Her brothers and sisters
were seals. And her real parents. They swam
all day together and at night slept upright
with their noses at the surface for air. I said
she never meant to lose this. But she wanted
to know what it felt like to be lost.
So some nights, while her family slept,
she left the water. On land her pelt was heavy,
like stewed velvet, so she taught herself
to take it off. Without it she looked
like a woman. She ran up and down the beach.
She saw seagulls, sand fleas, an osprey
hunting fish. For her the land was what remains
when the sea goes missing: the driftwood
remembered the water, the sand in the ground
remembered the ocean floor. Her body
always remembered her pelt. Except
of course, one night it wasn't there.
She searched everywhere, along the tideline,
over the dunes. When the sun came up

she slept under a boardwalk, and each night
she searched again. Until she found, not her pelt,
but the first child, me, tucked like a whisper
in the inner furl of a shell, then the second
folded in a morning glory, and the third asleep
with the ghost crabs in the dunes. And then,
because she loved us, she stopped searching.
I don't know why I said this. Maybe I saw her
looking at the ocean with an expression
I couldn't name. But then I forgot it, until one day,
maybe a year later, my sisters led me to the beach.
They were crying. They said they'd looked
and looked and finally found her sealskin,
and they'd decided to give it to her, even though
she might then swim away. And there it was.
There it was. A dried bundle. Maybe cardboard.
But just like a pelt would be after ten or so years
in the sand. For a moment I thought I could
fix this. I told them I had lied. But they just
looked out at the ocean. At the pelicans
dropping like weights. At the water
stretched out over nothing. And there was
no seal. There was no seal family. Just the waves
pressing higher and higher up onto the shore.

Redshift

When the search party finds
our neighbor, she is still
in the lake, in her nightgown,
her hands like cold flowers at her wrists.
I go to school anyway. On a test
I write down everything I know
about the Doppler effect, how objects
phase to red as they hurtle away.
In the hills above town the aircraft
warning lights are a family of throats
swallowing the same red bead of a word.
Don't say *suicide*. Don't say *never*
coming back. I learn that my sister
draws a dot on a neighborhood map
each time someone dies. A constellation
taking shape like the glow-in-the-dark
stars above our beds. I don't picture
our neighbor jumping, but sometimes
I imagine her sitting up at night.
She's not the only one. Last year her son
tossed a cord over the soft bark of a tree.
My other sister had a friend who took off alone,
thirteen years old and driving angry

up into the hills. In my family
we can't ask *what if one of our own.*
Fears come alive in the speaking of them.
The same surge could trip us all.

Shelter

At the edge of the piney woods lived a father
who loved his children so much he rigged
bear traps in a circle around the yard—not
to keep his children in, but to keep danger out.
To make up for the loneliness, he gave them each
a goat, slat-eyed and calm. But the children
were soon desperate for more. He'd see them
on the porch, prying apart the blue flowers
that twist themselves shut at night. They spent hours
by the dead raccoon caught in one of the traps:
grubs in its sides, belly split open, bones showing
through the skin. They hunted small snakes
in the garden and cut them lengthwise to study
the slackened mice. At night the father
could hear them talking about what death looked like.
Then one day they found a white-tailed deer
twenty feet up in a tree, its hide sloughing off
in long strips. This was just beyond the yard.
Nearby they found blood in the dirt, a beaten patch
of grass where something huge had slept,
the prints of a big cat circling the traps. They decided
on a plan. At sunset they tied the oldest goat
to a bush. They gave it a plate of berries.

Then they sat on the porch and waited,
flashlights dark in their shaking hands. From bed
their father heard the goat. Of course he thought
it was one of his children. He ran outside
and saw everything, the pet tethered by the traps,
the blankets on the porch. He checked
on his children—they were in bed sleeping,
fully clothed, so he went to the goat.
It was terrified. He untied it, rubbed its forehead,
walked it back to the barn. Later the children woke
and saw the goat was missing. They ran to their father
and told him what they'd done. This time
he could fix it. He led them to the barn,
the goat alive in its stall. But that night,
while they slept, he killed a chicken and strung it
on a rope out in the woods. When the mountain lion
came to smell the carcass, he shot it. Then
went home and made oatmeal for the children,
sat at the table and said nothing while they ate.

Hotel Sisters

We listen to each radio station drop
    off the edge of its town,
        then buzz in the dark stretches,

and we take turns scrying the dial
    for a clear tune to dance to. Our way
        of saying, *Look at us,*

we're all grown up. But each time
    we strike gold in the airwaves,
        I picture our car overturned

on the road, one wheel
    still spinning, the speakers flooding
        that same eternal pop song

over the asphalt: *We love each other,*
    we lose each other, we can't
        let each other go. All the bargains

of the universe on loop
    in the static and grind. In secret
        we've always called each other

by the radio alphabet signs for our initials:
Echo, Sierra, and Juliett Hotel,
names to flare above bad weather.

Our mother has pulled us each
separately aside and said,
Your sisters will be with you

for the long haul, meaning, *Learn*
to hold on to these guttering girls.
What else could I ever do? Someday

one of us will be the last one left.
Until then, each blaze of approaching headlights
shows me their faces, live and gold.

Flight Path

1

This one is not about the man who washed ashore.
It's about the girls who found him. From the dunes
they thought he was a beached porpoise. Later,
they pulled the sargassum from his chest
in bristled strips, brushed away the small crustaceans,
and placed clamshells over his mouth and his eyes.
Then they dug a moat around him and stayed
until it filled. This took all night. They'd never seen
the waves so dark before. They'd never realized that stars
rotate past their apexes and fall back toward the earth.
All night little shells gasped up from the ground
then suckered down again. The wind tugged sand
in layers over the beach like a veil. As the moat filled
the man rose slowly. The girls backed away from him
onto the drying sand. They wouldn't speak for days
and then only questions. Where had he come from?
Who had he loved? Would other men follow
after him? They could see right through his body,
the twin squids of his lungs filled with brine,
his eel intestines, mollusk spleen. They carried this
with them, long after the tide took him back.

2

Our great-grandfather was a test pilot.
We don't know much.
The engine sputtered just after takeoff?
The plane corkscrewed down to the earth?
In a single-seat interceptor fighter
he would have been able to feel the engine
choke on its pistons and then give up.
Let's say the propeller slows enough
for him to see the wood blades turning.
Let's say the right wing drops.
The horizon flips, then steadies,
flips again. In the tiny cockpit
he slides the canopy bubble aft
but doesn't eject. Then the nose hits earth.
The propeller slashes up a line of sod.
The engine smashes back into the fuel tank.
Behind the fireproof bulkhead
he hurtles from his seat. For a moment
he's airborne—no fuselage, no windscreen,
just his Army Air Corps uniform
against the sky—then he dies on his back

twenty yards away from the wreckage,
where the fabric wings flare and wilt
across their aluminum frames.

3

We went down to the beach
one night, my sisters and I,
to scare the ghost crabs, which drown
in water and suffocate in air.
We shined flashlights
into their coin-sized holes
and sometimes a claw glittered
then pulled back. When we turned
our lights off, a hundred of them
charged to the water to wet
their gills and breathe.
On their way back the seagulls
were waiting. Not all of the crabs
made it through. I didn't know then
what to call this—
the crabs daring the gulls
to take them, believing
or pretending they'd survive.

4

The man had been born on an island.
He had a wife there, the girls decided,
some children, and a little dog. Even so,
he raided the gull nests along the cliff
for feathers. He carved a lightweight frame
from driftwood. He split the sides of beehives
for their wax. The finished wings
were gray and white and as lovely
as he'd imagined. He fixed them to his arms
with twine. He dove from a cliff.
At first he dropped toward the water,
but then he learned to push the air behind him
and started gaining height. He'd expected this,
and to feel his heartbeat in his fingers,
and to see his shadow on the waves below.
But there were parts he hadn't considered.
The muscles in his back were not used
to this effort. He hadn't thought the wind
would be so loud. Nor had he imagined
the earth's wide curve at its edges,
the whales silhouetted in the bay,
the updrafts, how sore his arms
would become, and the rim of darkness

where the shallow water drops into depth.
When he fell it was over this darkness.
He was so tired, the girls said,
what else was there to do?
His family watched from the beach.
The feathers floated in slowly. His children
gathered them for a while, a day,
a week, a year, and then went away.

5

They weren't surprised by the telegram,
were they, our grandmother and her older brother,
Frank—they knew that danger circles right
where you expect it, but they hadn't thought ahead
to what came next, the fact that he stayed away,
the silent dinners, how their mother now
stood in their doorways and wished them goodnight,
the new expression on her face, the plates stacked
in labeled boxes, the move to a smaller house,
the table's empty seat that moved with them,
the report cards, the bicycles, the birds that returned
after winter, the country returning to war.

6

If he had noticed the engine clicking as he taxied // if he had
tightened the throttle friction nut to keep from stalling during the
climb // if he had kept his right wing level when the propeller
slowed // if he had used the rudder pedals to stabilize the yaw
// if he had raised the ailerons // if he had parachuted out into
the silence // if he had a parachute at all // if he had worn
his safety harness // if he had carried a rabbit's foot or a silver
charm // if he had been somehow different // returned to his
children // been felled years later by a 20mm cannon or flak
over Cologne // or if the sea and not the sky had called him //
if he had left his family for a gray-hulled submarine // if it had
filled one night in freezing waters // if he had not chosen to be
careless with a body that someone else loved //

7

I found Sierra on the fire escape.
Our whole family has the story wrong.
I pulled my head back through the window
and stood against the wall. She said,
Any test pilot would have known
that if your engine fails and you bank like that,
there's no way to maintain lift. I could still see her,
hand in her coat pocket, foot propped on a rung.
I was there to drive her home. She said,
Sometimes crashing feels like the only way out.
In a window across the alley a man washed dishes.
Someone else turned on a TV. That night I dreamed
a plane plummeted to the ocean. I was the search party.
The fuselage burned so hot I could see right through
into the cockpit where a young woman sat
impossibly aflame, like a keyhole, or
an exit, or a torch into the tunnel-end of risk.

8

The man was falling again, this time

through water. The tide had finally

brought him far enough out to sea.

First he fell through the sunlit regions.

Through mats of seaweed, schools of dolphins,

past turtles, past solitary sharks. As he fell

he grew even more transparent, the girls said,

which is what happens after you fly too close

to the sun. The water grew colder.

The light grew purple. Sometimes,

the girls said, there's no light down there

at all. He fell past swordfish in this twilight

and past wolf eels. His organs cast

dim shadows on the clear walls of his skin.

As he fell he fed the ones that lived there.

Suckers latched on to him. Teeth came

and ribboned him away. By now the water

was near freezing. He fell deeper,

his arms extended behind him like they had

in flight. He fell past glowing jellyfish,

past lanterneyes, past species, the girls said,

that over eons had invented their own light.

When he reached the bottom, the column

of water drove him into the sand.

Yet he lived: the scavengers

came to meet him, cat sharks, hagfish.

Worms found him. Limpets attached

to his bones. In the dark he was a landscape

of bacteria. He became a forest

of snails and clams. The girls made a list

of everything inside him.

They argued and added. Until in the end

each girl had a list of her own.

Keeping

One year, I think it was spring,
my sisters and I jacked the floorboards
off the foundation and sawed
the pipes from the walls,
then loaded the two-story house
on a wide-bed truck and drove.
When we found a hill no one
had built on, we dragged the frame
from the truck and set it down. Flush
against the earth. Nature entered
when we weren't watching. Grasses
pried through the floor, and scorpions
ferried their dim offspring
across the shelves. One morning
I opened a bedroom closet to find
a barn owl perched on the rod,
but by then I wasn't even surprised
by its porcelain face, my own
indoor moon. Or one of them,
because by then too I saw moons
everywhere, in the web-whorls
spiders left on the windows,
in the pale grubs curled in the dirt.

Our future, I thought, was like
a lunar eclipse: a shadow of a shape.
We took turns telling each other
about the mineshaft where children
might bathe after rainstorms,
slipping into the water like pale flames.
But no one came except, one day,
a woman from a wildlife rescue,
with foxes and owls and a faun.
When she opened the cages, they bolted.
She said this was how it always was:
first the caring, then the absence,
then the letting go. She left. It got dark.
We sat where the small farewell happened
and beamed a light toward the trees,
for eyeshine, spidershine, anything
to say the land was looking back.

Big Blue

Let's be honest: I'm far from home now,
nostalgic for an animal I've never

actually seen, and lying below the copy
suspended in the Hall of Ocean Life.

He's my dirigible, tethered, untested.
His cables hum in the frequency

I'm tuned to, cast geometric ripples
between us on the floor. As a child

I spread the *National Geographic*
across my parents' bed to learn

just how small a diver could look
beside another breathing mammal,

then watched myself in the mirror
shrinking that small in the live glass.

I sang a tune that ended *and way out there*
in outer space, Pluto takes his final place.

We are and are not so many things.
His eye might be as tall as I am.

Figure-Ground Illusion

Sometimes I want to say
the rest of our lives, but what if
he startles like a rabbit in the brush

*

want to say that together
we could be two words
the sort that hold hands
but still keep their original meanings
like *life* and *boat*

*

and sometimes I'm the whole
observable universe
the rest of the map uncharted
except for my face in the mirror
whose lips might be saying
the opposite of mine

*

but when we're walking in a field
and see an eagle

I just talk about its eyes
how they readjust to focus
on the animal, not the ground

Elegy for an Origin Point

My mother calls—she's had the dream
again, the one where our first dog,
Ivy, has left and taken up with another
dog in the woods, and my mother
wants to make sure she is happy,
so she sits by the stream until finally
Ivy and this other dog pass through,
and it's like seeing the unicorn
from the medieval tapestries, faun-footed,
wild, except this unicorn is Ivy
and she's glad, briefly, to be found,
to have her downy temples rubbed while
the strange dog waits to the side, to have
her flank scratched again by my mother
before slipping back, untethered,
into the world that she made hers.

Lamarckian Inheritance

All that has been acquired or altered in the organization
of individuals during their life is preserved by generation,
and transmitted to new individuals which proceed from
those which have undergone these changes.

—JEAN-BAPTISTE LAMARCK

The tumor was the size of a small-
    caliber bullet.
  A pair of blue gloves
probed her slick ridges,
      pink fields,
    gray hills that I love,
    and found it

in a layer of brain
    called the *dura mater.*
  Tough mother.
I've never touched the scar—
    we're too close
    for this kind of intimacy—
    so I don't know

how the old theory works,
    do I inherit the scar,

the tumor, the history
behind it? We're all steeped
in the tragedies
of our parents' generation.
Take the doctor's hands

in JFK's bloody hair. My mother
sometimes calls this
her *claim to fame*,
that her neurosurgeon used to work
in Dallas, was in Trauma
Room One that day.
I'm such a selfish little nation—

in my version of the story,
it's all leading up to
my mother and to me,
how we sometimes lie in hammocks
late at night and watch
the sky fall toward us
through its glittery sieve.

Her doctor insisted once
his president stay
clothed, for dignity,
through all of it, the crash cart,
the inspection for fatal
wounds. How is it that
a puncture

can be mistaken, can be buried
by hair, by a flap of scalp,
can be an entrance
or an exit depending on the light,
why, sooner
or later, are holes punched
through everything?

Still Life

It was not a very small goat. Its ears turned delicately to its own tapping across the tiles and its creased nose smudged the frames of the larger paintings. It stayed often with the portraits. Looked up at the sad women draped thinly on the walls. When it slept it arranged its bony knees around itself in a wreath and sank its nose in the tufted balloon of its belly. It never hurt anything except once when it took the title *Nostalgia in Blue* from a kitchen scene of a mother pouring milk and laid this with careful teeth below a study of irises. Perhaps that was its idea of a joke. It walked scratchy and brown through the wide galleries and the long empty halls. It got cold. It turned its back on the quiet ballerina and breathed along with the saints. It blinked with horizontal pupils at its own reflection in the marble floor but did not know itself and walked across the glassy yellow eyes. In one hall there was a painting of a goat hanged with a rope. The soft V of its neck strained against the canvas.

Cassandra

It's time to leave again. She unplugs the fridge
and watches until the orange coils on its back
have faded down to gray. She turns off the gas.
She papers the windows in layers from the outside,
because if she doesn't, the moon will reflect in them
like a lamp in every room. And then the house will still
seem lived in. And then how to move on?
The last thing she does, always, is go with them
one by one into their rooms and hold them up
to pluck the glow-in-the-dark stars from the ceiling.
They place the stars inside a wooden box. Which
is what they are, her children, little hinged boxes
full of a chemical that makes light out of nothing,
that glows all on its own. They're wearing coats
over their patterned pajamas. When the stars are away
the house is completely dark, and somehow the sounds
are louder, the final shut of the door, the porch steps,
the frogs like small rocks clacking in the trees'
throats. In the yard's farthest corner, she asks
her children what they can see. As always, they say,
Nothing. The house could be invisible. It could
have shrunk to the size of a blackberry. The hill
could have grown up to swallow it. It might have

changed into a tree. She's relieved. She can still see it
so clearly, like the retinal burn of a lightbulb long after
it's been turned off. Like all their other houses,
the already and the not-yet, ranged like old flares
across the hills. She starts walking and her children follow.
They're kicking up moss in a trail for the night to erase.
They're mimicking a screech owl, then listening,
because if they call in the right voice something may
call back. Before long they'll be climbing the hill
to the new house, opening the unlocked door,
claiming bedrooms. Then waiting for her to reattach
the constellations, asking, *Is this a cat? a cave?*
a sleeping bear? a little spoon? And they won't know.
And she won't be able to correct them.
And soon she'll unwrite the stars again, and they'll go on.

Canopy

All year Juliett's bedroom ceiling leaks brown water,
but since the drip never falls from the same place long
she rearranges her furniture to escape it. Her bed
is first against one wall and later another, her desk
looks out the small window and then does not.
When the sheetrock finally cracks, her nightstand
is what's ruined. Her lamp, her clock, the triptych
of family photos she took when she moved.
Her landlord says he'll investigate. For days, nothing,
then finally, he calls: the people living above her
covered their floor in soil and planted trees.
The next day she sees them in the stairwell,
shrunken pines, their bald roots wrapped in plastic—

Old Flares

It was easier to leave than I pretended,
night-lit city falling away below,

but for years I've kept my radio tuned
to the hometown channel, in case of something, fire,

earthquake, the need again to go. And it's played
through static: today, a man from the public gardens

says he can't believe the fish just disappeared.
At first he thought they were hiding, but—

when he says missing, I repeat, *missing*. Stolen,
stolen. We used to feed them from the wooden bridge.

I call my sisters. I wash my empty car.
I read anything about the mystery I can find.

Mammoth Cave

In the main cavern, an LED-lit sign tells us
about the fish. Down here, in the longest
known cave system, creatures evolved
away from the light, went translucent,
grew skin back over their eyes. He says,
What are you thinking, and I say, *Love,* as in,
this version of me you love is only
the surface, pines and a damp June wind.
We're holding hands. I've been in a bad mood
since I practiced driving manual, and he saw
I can't clutch or shift gears. I thought,
maybe this is the reason he leaves me.
He suggested a trip to the national park.
I guess it's dangerous to love so skeptically,
but I've seen him ruthless—last winter,
the mice, how he set out pots
of oil-skinned water to drown them.
When I was eight, my grandfather had a stroke,
then stopped taking his blood thinners,
then had another stroke. That weekend
I saw my grandmother standing in the garage.
Her mouth had broken out

in terrible sores. The metal door was down,
leaving her backlit by a dim sliver. But I didn't
go to her. I stood in the dark and watched.

Long View

The old motel is still there
in the dunes, and the oil rig
still flickers like a deserted city
on the horizon. When we check in,
the receptionist says that long ago
a woman swam all the way to the rig
from shore. Someone else told us
this story when we were children:
the empty city doesn't give up
its first inhabitant easily, so like grief
the swimmer has to settle in. She scales
the derrick, tears her clothes
into strips and ties them to the cables,
presses her face against the warm
engine's side. It's getting late,
but we leave our bags in the room
and follow the boardwalk
to the beach, where the waves
touch shore in little habitual apologies
and the sand holds our footprints
like it's never been walked on before.
We play our old game, count
the lights: the moon, the safety beams

on the oil rig, swathe of galaxy,
phosphorescing shrimp. The beach
is so bright, it could be day
on a different planet, a dimmer one,
farther from the sun—making us
very far away, looking around
at an array of distant lights
and signaling straight
for the small blue earth: *Do not
miss us*, we say, and, *We're sorry*,
sorry we left with no note
or explanation, you see,
we always intended to come back.

Echo Hotel

*

You watch your high beams cut an arc through asteroidal dust.
You eat a peach going dry at its pit. You rotate again the three-
dimensional constellations on your map, swing your feet onto
the console, and lean back in the narrow chair, your eyes on
the canopy bubble of titanium-reinforced glass. *This is it, folks,*
you say into the star-stitched quilt of deep space—the field of
crumbling asteroids, the nebulas clustered like moths along the
galaxy's bright spine. You say it again and picture the light from
your solo pod dispersing outward with nothing to stop it. You
notice a quick streak of yellow ahead and have to tell yourself it's
not a ship, even though you memorized the probability equation
like everyone else: where N is the chance of being found again
once separated, let N equal one over *the visibility of your vessel*
times *your last known distance from the vessel you lost* times
the size of the universe times *the fraction of your human life
remaining* times *the estimated inadequacy of your maps*. But you
never listen, do you, and that little button of hope springs up in
your sternum no matter how many times it's been pressed.

*

The spiraled eel of the galaxy opened its mouth and said, *Enter*, and your many-times-great-grandparents followed in star ships named for the wonders they left behind, which in turn became your wonders, the monumental engine room on the SS *Sahara*, the hanging curtains of wheat in *Amazon*'s aeroponic fields, the gilded theater on *Blue Sky* brought in panel by panel, a teacher once told you, from an already-antique theater on Earth. You spent those early school cycles trying to imagine it: life on a planet where the asterisms stayed fixed in an endless rotation, where for half the hours one yellow star prospered at the expense of the rest. You saw the old constellations once, in a ceiling mosaic on *Pacific* before it vanished from the Flotilla during a magnetic storm. The mosaic was created just after the venture, or the exodus, or the evacuation, while the last great cartographers charted the galaxy using the one distance sensor they had left. The teacher gathered your class around him and pointed out the shapes: hunter wielding his laser array, small bear blundering up a mountain, cluster of sisters gripping each other tightly in case the darkness tries to tear them apart.

*

Your first time piloting a solo pod was like a dream of falling:
everything in the galaxy narrowed to one dark chute. Your shift
commander told you to expect this, and after the flight session he
stood you and the other trainees against the hangar wall, saying,
At least one of you will get dazzled by that emptiness and forget
to turn back. Everyone knew what followed: you'll fall from sight
range. When this happens, the watchposts have no choice but to
mark you as lost. Your mother had gone silent when you signed
up for flight patrol, and your father still kept finding reasons
to avoid your gaze. That first night after training, the rooms
you shared were empty, the radio left on low volume beside the
couch. Your father's voice came out of it. *This is it, folks, just the*
midsized comet to report. You hadn't realized he was on duty.
From his post he would have seen a swarm of taillights shrinking
against the steady field of stars, then a moment of darkness, then
thirteen sets of high beams as the shift commander called you
back. Unlike your father, you've seen the Flotilla from a distance.
When you turned around it was tiny, a wreath of shadows
specked in light.

*

You have enough food to last two years on the old solar calendar
and an aeroponics chamber to grow more. You have a fuel
recycler. A cot. A case of palm-sized books. You press a detective
novel twice, for sound only, and the librarian reading it has the
soft accent of someone only a generation or two removed from
Earth. While *the gumshoe takes his dame for a spin in the clip
joint* she sounds tender, but when *the trouble boys throw lead in
an alley* her voice goes rough. As she speaks, the book lights up,
noting that *lead* was a form of weapon in the old days and a *dame*
was the female equivalent of a knight. You pause the recording
and sit in the darkness, trying not to think of yourself as the
human equivalent of night. You fall asleep with the navigation on
auto and wake to the sound of your radio muttering the signature
of a nearby star. The low-pitched etch of its wavelength could
be saying, *Please.* Or, *Seize.* When it quiets, you imagine your
family's persistent whisper, and *Tundra's*, carrying them. You
turn on all the books at once to drown it out. *What have we done,*
a romance novel says in a dead librarian's voice. *What do we do,*
says a memoir a moment later.

*

As a child you had night terrors. Sometimes the star ship was a wood-paneled labyrinth that you'd never get out of. Sometimes you fell deeper into nothing. Sometimes you were drowning in a vertical column of wheat. You always woke to your father asking, *Are you back now?* When you nodded, he'd hand you shoes, a jacket, and a vacuum flask of tea. That late, the corridor lights were lowered to simulate nightfall, so you could barely see the slick grooves worn in the floor by ten generations of footsteps. You'd go sit under the cottonwoods in the oxygen-generator, or play a round in the arcade, or stand in the library pressing book after book until the shelves echoed with ancient voices telling stories. On the nights of your worst terrors, he'd take you to the aqua tanks, where your mother monitored the pressure and acidity of the coral reef. She'd be wearing her battered white oxy-suit and walking slowly across the sand, and when she noticed you, she saluted with her right glove. But once she was hacking at a chalk-gray branch of coral and didn't see you. Bubbles rose from her torch-saw. A school of silver fish parted around her. You stood at the glass and willed her to sense you until your father took you away.

*

One night your father brought you to *Tundra's* outward
watchpost. He'd told you about it, of course, the five old
telescopes pivoting in algorithmic patterns, the watchers behind
them strapped into their chairs, above them the largest glass
dome in the Flotilla, and beyond, a wild swathe of stars. But
you'd never been there. The watchers were trading stories about
the handful of people who'd been lost and made their way back.
They seemed surprised to learn your father had a child, but one
offered you her telescope to have a look. As you strapped in, she
kept talking about the hull welder who returned while she was
on duty. His pod had blown out of sight in a solar wind, she said,
and he navigated back by tuning his emergency radio to the
occasional hint of a song. You'd heard this story before, but not
the next part: he swore that he'd seen giant creatures grazing on
dark matter, and that each moon wore the same face. Your father
patted your back and said, *That's why we watch for stragglers.*
You looked through the black rubber eyepiece. The whole galaxy
burst and bloomed and, stunned by brightness, you almost
thought you saw it: a tiny blue orb like the coin of light at the top
of a very deep shaft.

*

Your uncle said the seas rose and flooded everything. The ship's librarian told you there had been a terrible war. Your teachers suggested you think of it as a great museum burned down, as a library gone missing. All were careful not to cast it as a home abandoned, so you took a while to define this feeling you were born with as grief. When you finally did, you told your parents there was a hole in your chest the size of a planet. They looked at each other. That night, they took you to the inward watchpost, pointed at the fleet, and said, *To stay human you have to remember everything we have left.* But the ships looked to you like whales in an ocean. And you heard their words differently: *To stay human you have to remember everything we have left.* Which is why you listen to the books that remember forests. Dive bars. Cars stalled on bridges. Horses galloping down roads. How the air felt before it was recycled. What it was like to stand on ground that slowly spun. Each time a book ends, you light a flare and hope someone will see you. You think of the bright little fish in the aqua tank. Of the watchers pivoting slowly beneath their spectacular dome. Of your parents bereft in their apartment. All of you so small and so far from home.

Archipelago

In the family photo, the three of us are standing
on beach chairs dragged way out into the surf,

looking at the waves, not at the camera. This
must have been the summer we found the book

of deep-sea creatures no one knew existed
until they washed ashore dead, and we were afraid

of everything unknown and known, monsters, crabs,
the stingrays with those barbs that are so hard

to remove. These days, our grandmother cries
for everyone she ever lost, as if they all died

yesterday. I can only imagine this kind of grief
and I do. I'm still in the part of my life

before the loss I won't get over. And when
will it be. And who. And look at us. An island chain

of sisters above frill sharks, bristlemouths, the black
swallower, the gulper eel with its impossible jaw.

This Time

Sierra's walking the train tracks behind
her rented house, calling each of us: Juliett in Austin,
me even farther, our parents in New Mexico
where the sky fades to purple, they say, just before
it rains. She's working on a farm that rescues horses.
Today she led a bay named Quincy out of his stall.
He'd been a small-time racehorse before
he came to her, and when she unclipped the lead rope
in the pasture, he took off running like it was the only way
he knew to be in the world—whinnying, bucking,
tossing his head. Then there was a sound
she didn't recognize, and he was lurching toward her,
head low over the grass. When he reached the fence
he slammed against a post. When the post fell
he fell with it. Then heaved himself over the brambles.
Then crawled across the road, shredding his knees
on the asphalt, trailing blood. On the other side
he stood and careened into the sparse woods.
That's when she knew he was dying. She followed,
his witness, who used to beg our parents to kill anything
accidentally hurt, the moth touched with a wet hand,
the mouse flung against a door. Later, when Quincy
was still, the vet would place a finger to show where

his neck broke when he tossed his head in the field.
Broke, but didn't quite sever the cord.
So he could keep running, through the woods and on
to a street lined with houses, his hooves loud
on the driveways and quiet over the lawns.
He shoved his head through a kitchen window.
He ran to the soccer field and knocked over a goal.
When Sierra caught up, he was tangled,
breathing so hard the mesh rose and fell with his ribs.
She should have let him stop there. Instead,
a thousand miles away from me, she braced her feet
in the grass and lifted the net.

Experiment

Once I set fire
to a scrap of paper,

dropped it in a glass
milk bottle, and

plugged the mouth
with a peeled egg.

When the air was spent
the bottle became

a vacuum. Then
finally, constricted

by the pressure,
the egg's ashen belly

fell. The bottle
gasped. I am not strong.

I am not strong, not
permanent, just holding.

Jaws

I don't realize I'm starved
for the color until the blood

washes up on the beach.
I'm craving red but still

haven't seen the creature,
just the quick whip and slither

of its tail in the wake
—and then there I am,

facing the skin side
of the animatronic shark.

The slick apertures of its eyes.
The mythic teeth.

The anvil nose beating
the deck, cracking windows.

The shark, like the moon, is
pockmarked, unstoppable,

never showing its hidden side.

Surely space is just another underwater,

the messages we send from satellites
a bleeding haze of infrared:

This is my blood type,
this is where I keep my body at night,

and I tell no one about the times
my body, taking over,

stands waist-deep in the surf,
some wild need inside me

ticking into place.

Scenic Overlook on the
Rio Grande Gorge

The ground is flatlining.
He walks to the edge. From the car,
I pretend I'm a statue
in a roadside altar, minor saint
spun backwards into clay. My job,
always, to watch the supplicants
through their motions of grief: nails torn
at the roots, hair strewn.
Someday my parents will want
to have their ashes scattered here,
which is a strange thing to know.
He's standing still, and I jolt again—
my geologic pang,
my mile-deep rift with joy
at the bottom, flash of river
between the sharp rocks. We say
I love you all the time, text it, spell it out
in fingertips on each other's backs.
There's a point not too far
down the road where the gorge
disappears from sight.

Even though she's grown up,
my sister still presses her thumb
into that soft nest of veins where her clavicle
branches, the jugular notch, which she says
is the part of her body that has always felt
most vulnerable. When she was little
she'd hold her hand there and ask,
with terror, if it was possible to scoop
her throat out with a spoon. Me,
I dream about hands ripping my jaw
from my skull, leaving just upper teeth
and a tongue flopping below.
Maybe we all have secret places
where the potential damage feels most real.
It's almost mythological. Over ninety years ago,
my great-grandmother nursed her baby,
my grandmother, under a tree.
She heard a noise and looked up.
A foot-long centipede was falling toward her
from a branch, its back-plates twisting.
She moved the baby's head
and the creature, segmented and heavy,
landed on her exposed breast.

It latched and unlatched.
For the rest of her life she had a centipede-
shaped scar. Someday I'll have a baby
with a groove in her head for her brain
to bloom toward, a sweet spot you could push
your thumb into and ruin for life.

I Wake Up in a Painting

This time
he, the sleeping figure, I, the lion,
my pupils round in their egg-whites,
night-wind

angling his scent
dunewards. He has surprised me.
I never expected a human in the sand
like a god fallen

asleep,
a book still open on the pillow
beside him. I smell the creased shoulder
of his robe.

Don't know
which path he took across the desert.
On the nightstand we keep a lamp,
a vase,

               a digital clock.
Beneath the blue walls I hold the moon
in my teeth and breathe on it, feel no
             devouring dread.

Owl

One day you and I will have a house
together. We'll drink wine by the stove
and leave the kitchen door open

to let in the night. Until one evening
a barn owl flies in through the door.

He'll perch on the fridge and look down
from beside the bottles, his face
round and clean as a dish. You'll know

what to do. You'll turn off the lights,
the music, the blue flame. I'll open

the windows. We'll find an old blanket
and sit on the porch, and we'll listen
to our house become wild. It will sound

like the owl is asking, *When is it due?*
When is it due? I'll expect him

to miss the stars, but you won't be surprised

when he chooses to stay. That night,

when the wind picks up, you'll tell me

about a woman your grandparents knew,

who taught her parrot to sing

in her dead husband's voice. Again

and again, the same tune: *How*

can this be true? How can this be true?

Incantation for If and When I Lose Him

He makes a good
decommissioned warship,
I make a good ocean,

good tugboat leading him
far enough from the shore,
good explosive fixed in rows

below the waterline of his hull.
This series of hollow booms
is our last slow dance—

when I have flooded
all his rooms, the empty bunks,
the engine stripped of its wires,

let his portholes fill
and fall like plunder,
let him stay where I sink him.

Let the fish come, let the coral
turn this wreck and tender
into something new.

Spell

My mother calls to tell me a story.
She and my father were driving
on a mountain road, and all around,
the aspen trees were dying—
each one on the mountainside leafless,
clutching a sticky gold web in its branches
like it had caught a rotten cloud.
Where the road turned along a cliff
the guardrail was missing.
Far below, a red pickup truck
lay wedged between two rocks.
They got out their binoculars. The doors
were pinned shut. The paint was fresh.
It must, she says, have been two
hundred, three hundred feet down.
Phones didn't work on the mountain.
They stood in the road for a moment
then got back in the car and drove away.
What else was there to do?
When they rounded the turns
they were careful. When they found
a gas station they told the cashier
what they'd seen. He laughed,

said the truck had crashed a year ago
but was too far down the gorge
to pull back up. He'd been working
the night it happened. No headlights,
no motor, then suddenly, a woman
laced with scratches walked in from the road.
She'd climbed out the rear windshield
and scrambled downhill. Then
my father asked, *What's going on
with the aspens?* So the cashier
told them about the webworms
and the trees. The aspens only look
dead, he said, because their branches
have been chewed clean. When the air
goes cold, the worms will drop
to the ground and cocoon there,
and in spring, moths will fly up
from the dirt. And this is the world
my parents are finally proud to give me,
here in a tale where everybody lives:
a red truck in flight over a mountain,
landing gently; moths about to open
like white flowers; empty-handed
trees about to fill again with leaves.

All the Old Answers

When my great-uncle died, his children
held the wake in the old house,
the house he had grown up in, inherited,
and condemned in his will. He wanted
his house's story to end when his did.
This was a selfishness I understood.
I'd read somewhere that no structure
is ever really finished, not while shingles
are still loosening into their rough patterns,
walls still learning the level of the earth.
While a building stands, anything
can happen in it: any pipe can leak,
any stranger break through a kitchen window
on a summer night. At the wake,
a cousin-once-removed told stories
about her father, and in every story
he was a different kind of man.
Then we took flashlights up to the attic,
where we found a trunk of military coats.
Pine marten skins in a plastic hatbox.
Old wooden bed frames. A dozen
amateur portraits of a liver-and-white dog.
In a corner was a tiny dollhouse

shaped like the house we stood in,
down to the palm-sized rugs. Under a sheet
was a buffalo skull that looked so ragged,
the animal might have died during the first years
of slaughter, back when no one thought
the wild could ever disappear, back when
grasshoppers moved across the plain
like a cloud, stripping everything,
grass from the ground, fur from the animals'
throats. It's as good as any other way
to think of history, a legion of beating creatures
that seem, from a distance, like one great storm.
I covered the naked skull with its sheet.
I looked on the back of each portrait
in case the dog had a name. I took the dollhouse
for my future children. They'll move
the little figures from room to room.

Notes

"Selkie" borrows its narrative and syntactical structure, as well as the phrases "What was the harm?" and "But there was no . . . ," from Brigit Pegeen Kelly's "Black Swan" in *The Orchard* (BOA Editions, 2004).

"Lamarckian Inheritance" refers to Jean-Baptiste Lamarck's disproven theory of evolution. The epigraph is taken from Henry Fairfield Osborn's translation of Lamarck's 1815 *Histoire Naturelle* in *From the Greeks to Darwin* (Macmillan, 1894).

"Mammoth Cave" borrows the phrase *"What are you thinking*, and I say . . ." from B. H. Fairchild's "Beauty" in *The Art of the Lathe* (Alice James Books, 1998).

Acknowledgments

Many thanks to the editors of these journals and publications, in which versions of the following poems have appeared:

32 Poems: "Mammoth Cave"

Arts & Letters: "Distortion for Afterward"

Colorado Review: "All the Old Answers" and "Keeping"

Copper Nickel: "Spell"

Gulf Coast: "A Circling" (originally titled "Lamarckian Inheritance II")

Hayden's Ferry Review: "Still Life"

Mississippi Review: "Redshift"

Missouri Review: "Selkie" and "Still" (originally titled "Dipping Achilles")

The Offing: "Archipelago," "Experiment," and "Incantation for If and When I Lose Him"

Painted Bride Quarterly: "Red Planet" and "I Wake Up in a Painting"

The Paris Review: "Young Relics" and "Cassandra"

Radar Poetry: "Spring Break at Port Aransas"

The Southern Review: "Shelter" and "Owl"

"Distortion for Afterward" received the 2014 Rumi Prize in Poetry from *Arts & Letters.*

"Still" was a finalist for the 2017 Jeffrey E. Smith Editors' Prize from the *Missouri Review.*

Gratitude

Thank you, first, to Ken Hine, Shannon Kilgore, Sarah Hine, and Jessie Hine. What more can I say? All my love and gratitude forever.

Thank you to the rest of my family, here and gone, for being family and for telling stories.

Thank you to Sarah Gorham and Jeffrey Skinner for seeing this book so clearly and bringing it to life. Thanks to Sarah, further, for her impeccable and wise edits, to Alban Fischer for making real the cover of my dreams, and to the entire team of Sarabandits for everything they've done and continue to do.

Thank you to Jen Benka, Mary Gannon, and the staff at the Academy of American Poets, for their leadership, compassion, and joy in poetry.

Thank you to Miriam Bailin, Melissa Gurley Bancks, Mary Jo Bang, Kimberly Horne, Major Jackson, Margaret Marcus, Sharon Olds, Jenny Xie, and more poets, teachers and professors than I can name, for being guiding lights to me and so many others. My particular thanks to Catherine Barnett and Deborah Landau for their wisdom, patience, and grace.

Thank you to Madeleine Barnes, Sarah Bird, Laura Cresté, Kate Doyle, Ryan Dzelzkalns, Victoria Kornick, Anna Kovatcheva, Maya Phillips, and Talya Zax for being generous readers and dear friends. This book couldn't have existed without any of them. All my gratitude, too, to the Potter family for making me feel so welcomed and loved, and to Tashween Ali, Mira Dickey, Ellie D'Onofrio, Lucy Holden, Mary Hollyman, Rachel Koren, and Jessica Kruger, for their abiding friendship.

Thank you to Hubble, my snuggly canine ball of trouble and light.

And, finally, thank you to Steve Potter, for always being my first reader, my closest editor, and my everything else.

Originally from Austin, Texas, **EMMA HINE** received a BA from
Washington University in St. Louis and an MFA from New York
University. Her poems have appeared in *32 Poems*, *Arts & Letters*,
Gulf Coast, *Hayden's Ferry Review*, the *Mississippi Review*, the
Missouri Review, *Ninth Letter*, *The Offing*, *The Paris Review*, and
The Southern Review. She is the recipient of the 2019 Kathryn A.
Morton Prize in Poetry.

SARABANDE BOOKS is a nonprofit literary press located in Louisville, Kentucky. Founded in 1994 to champion poetry, short fiction, and essay, we are committed to creating lasting editions that honor exceptional writing. For more information, please visit sarabandebooks.org.